Clara B

Teacher, Nurse, Leader

Dona Herweck Rice

Clara

Clara Barton helped others.

Clara's house

She helped her sick brother.

She helped young children learn.

Think and Talk

How does your teacher help you?

Clara

She helped women
earn better pay.

She helped men in the
army who were hurt.

She helped the Red
Cross overseas.

Clara

She started the Red
Cross at home.

American Red Cross

Clara made the world a better place.

Clara Helps

The piglet was in trouble.

"Do not worry," Clara said. "I will help you."

Civics in Action

Each of us can do things to help others. We can pick up trash. We can make a card for a sick person. There is a lot we can do.

1. Think about one thing you can do to help others.

2. Plan for how you will help.

3. Share your plan.